spanish sign language

Reading comprehension activities

G. J. Bawcutt

Harrap London

First published in Great Britain 1977
by GEORGE G. HARRAP & CO. LTD.
182 High Holborn, London WC1V 7AX

Reprinted: 1979

ISBN 0 245 52993 4

Set in Univers type by Harry Darton and Associates Limited
Printed and bound by David Green (Printers) Ltd, Kettering, Northamptonshire
Made in Great Britain

CONTENTS

Introduction   4

Notes on using this book   4

SPANISH SIGN LANGUAGE   6

Topics   54

Language patterns   55

Word list   56

INTRODUCTION

Spanish people are proverbially hospitable, especially to foreigners, and love conversation. They would rather show you the way to the Plaza Mayor, it seems, than put up a sign pointing to its whereabouts. And, of course, the Plaza has been there a long time so everybody is likely to know where it is anyway. If you don't you must be a stranger and therefore interesting to talk to. So . . .

However, you will often find a written sign easier to understand than a barrage of rapid Spanish that you may have difficulty in following.

The language on signs is useful not only as information you need but to help you recognize patterns of language which are typically Spanish.

Recognising language on signs can save student and tourist visitors much inconvenience and at the same time make their visit more interesting.

NOTES ON USING THIS BOOK

Although not every aspect of Spanish life is portrayed, a working cross section is represented.

The pictures are broadly grouped under the headings of accommodation and food, communications, general notices, pastimes, road and traffic signs, shops, and transport. Each section progresses from easy to harder material. Sometimes words may have spelling errors or lack accents and will need some explanation.

Lists of pictures as they relate to topic and language forms are given on page 54. You will also find a short word list after the picture section.

Possibilities

This material may be used in a number of ways. This is not an exhaustive list:
a) as part of an existing course.
b) as a source for discussion or essays.
c) as part of a Spanish civilisation course. Many photographs pose questions about their way of life.
d) as revision or 'topping up'.
e) as a familiarisation with Spain.
f) as background study.

g) as practical illustration of points of grammar.

h) the questions may be replaced by your own.

i) some situations may give you ideas for role playing, simulations or practical and group work.

j) in addition to the signs themselves other details in the pictures can be used as source material.

k) because we are concerned primarily with comprehension, testing and discussion can be in English or Spanish, written or oral.

Follow up

Much of the value of material of this sort depends upon the ingenuity of the teacher. Perhaps some of the ideas below may act as starters.

1. Make your own slides during your next visit. Use colour film. Project them onto a large screen or onto the wall for maximum impact and involvement.
   Use the students' pictures as well as yours.

2. Mount four or five pictures onto card and use them as story packs. Students invent stories or situations in Spanish or English.

3. Start a competition for the most interesting, boring, wordy, funny sign met during the school trip.

4. On a visit make a set of pictures or photographs using as many visual captions as possible. Fill in with taped commentary and sound effects.

(Photo number 84 by R. Savage; all others by author)

spanish sign language

You are in Spain. It is quite likely that among the first signs you meet will be road signs. Very few are bilingual in any way, even close to the frontier. You will not get a 'warming up' period to get used to them. In common with British road signs, however, they tend to be informational or warning signs.

ZONA DE ESTACIONAMIENTO LIMITADO

ZONA AZUL
DISCO OBLIGATORIO
DE 9H. A 20H.
EXCEPTO FESTIVOS

1 The centres of many Spanish towns, like Logroño here, contain too much traffic. Instead of using parking meters as we do they favour Blue Zones.
  1. What are these zones?
  2. When can you park your car?
  3. When can you not leave your car in a parking place?

2 You are leaving Alcázar de San Juan in La Mancha. Herencia is the next town.

    1.   a) What main road are the two towns on?
        b) What do you think the N indicates?
        c) What distance separates the two places?
        d) Is this figure in miles or kilometres?

Look at the two speed restriction signs. The 70 is surrounded by a red circle. On the other the 40 is grey and divided by a black line.

    2.   a) How fast can you go without breaking the law?
        b) What does the other sign tell you?

3 A roadmenders' hut in the middle of nowhere is daubed with a terse message

    1.   Is it:
        a) an advert for babies?
        b) the name of the place?
        c) a message to the roadmenders?
        d) a message to the public in general?
    2.   What does it say?

4 On some signs in La Mancha the phrase *un lugar de la Mancha* and a silhouette of a knight on horseback are included.

5 Villafranca de los Caballeros is the next town.
1. What do you think the name means, if anything?
2. How far away is it?
3. When you get there, which of the following might you need to enjoy yourself to the full?
   a) butterfly net
   b) saddle
   c) fishing rod
   d) a carton of shot-gun cartridges
   e) altimeter and compass
   f) climbing boots
   g) swimming costume
   h) a pack of cards
   i) tent
   j) puncture outfit
   k) face mask
   l) colour film
   m) skis

1. Which world famous book could the figure of the knight be taken from?
2. Which town are you approaching?
3. Has the car in front been parked:
   a) on the cart track?
   b) at the kerb side?
   c) on the pavement?
   d) on the cycle track?

6 These four children are hurrying past the entrance to this coaching inn for which reason?

a) they are late for lunch
b) there is a vehicle approaching
c) it is dangerous to loiter as the gate is in constant use by vehicles leaving and entering
d) they are having a running argument

7 All the direction signs point the same way except one.

1. What would you expect to see or find at *Centro Ciudad*?
2. How far away is:
   a) Zaragoza?
   b) Logroño?

AL PUERTO ABIÉRTO DE ONCALA

C 115
73 ARN

8 On the C115 road to Arnedo there is this notice.
   1. Which is the correct interpretation?
      a) Oncala is a sea port
      b) Oncala is a mountain pass
      c) It is a free port where you can buy things very cheaply
      d) It is a place where refugees can find safety
      e) It is a mountain pass open all the year round
      f) It is a pass that is sometimes snowed-up but at this time is open to traffic
   2. Can you find it on a road map? Which province is it in?

LLANTA METALICA

9 This road sign is black and white and is surrounded by a red circle.
   1. Does it mean that:
      a) all horse carts are prohibited?
      b) all dog carts are prohibited?
      c) only small carts are prohibited?
      d) only carts with metal rimmed wheels are prohibited?
   2. Why do you think it is on the right side of the road?

10 You have been cycling down this track to explore the woods down in the valley when you come across this sign.

a) Is it some sort of crossing without a policeman?

b) Is it a warning of an ungated railway crossing?

c) Does it warn of no public right of way beyond this point, allowing only policemen to pass?

11 This sign is becoming much more familiar in Spain. The man in the distance is doing as he is told.

1. To whom is the sign directed?

2. What is it they are told to do?

12 You are in San Sebastián on the Basque sea coast. This sign is surrounded by a red circle.

1. Some people have apparently ignored the sign, but in what way?
2. Can you suggest a reason why they might be within their rights?
3. Name some of the jobs they might have.

13 Imagine that you are driving a large Pegaso lorry laden with coal in the port area of Bilbao. It is 9.15 p.m., you are tired at the end of a long day and you are looking forward to putting your head down as soon as possible.

1. Can you park your lorry in the lay-by here at this moment?
2. If not, can you park here at some other time?
3. When?

14

1. Which town is the bullfight being held in?
2. One of the boys is holding on to a 'No Parking' sign. Is it a permanent parking restriction or does it apply only sometimes? Give a reason for your answer.
3. Would you say the town was in the north, south, east or west of Spain?

15

Many Spanish road signs are similar to their British equivalent.

1. Does this one mean:
   a) You are allowed to park?
   b) You are not allowed to park?
2. Two people have parked their vehicles below a sign which says:
   a) Please keep clear
   b) Special parking bay
   Which is correct?
3. You are in a town called Teruel. What clue tells you this?

16 You have been stretching your legs in Logroño town centre and you notice another Blue Zone sign.

1. How do you account for the lack of times on this sign?
2. If you are heading in the direction of the elderly couple, where might you be going?
3. What might the notice be that the man in shirtsleeves is reading:
   a) a menu?
   b) rates of exchange?
   c) a bus time-table?
   d) tourist events information?
4. If you became a resident here, could you expect to open a savings account at this place?

17 To park in the Blue Zone you must obtain a control disc.

1. Where do you think you might obtain one?
2. Where should you place it?
3. For how long can you leave your car in a parking space without being fined?
4. What time must you leave?
5. How do you set the disc?

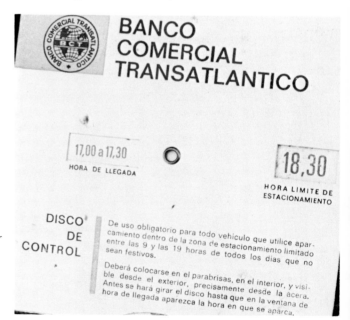

BANCO COMERCIAL TRANSATLANTICO

17,00 a 17,30
HORA DE LLEGADA

18,30
HORA LIMITE DE ESTACIONAMIENTO

DISCO DE CONTROL

De uso obligatorio para todo vehiculo que utilice aparcamiento dentro de la zona de estacionamiento limitado entre las 9 y las 19 horas de todos los dias que no sean festivos.

Deberá colocarse en el parabrisas, en el interior, y visible desde el exterior, precisamente desde la acera. Antes se hará girar el disco hasta que en la ventana de hora de llegada aparezca la hora en que se aparca.

Gran Camping Zarauz

2.ª CATEGORIA   N.º *2791*

D. *PERALTA*

Elem. de pago	Núm.	Precio por día	Importe por día
Adultos . .	2	25	50
Niños . . .			
Coche . . .	1	25	25
Moto . . .			
Bicicletas			
Autobús . .			
Caravana . .			
Tienda . .	1	25	25

Llegada *16-8*	Total por día	100
	x *1* días	100
Salida *17-8-71*	Total a pagar	100

18 Look at this bill for accommodation at the Gran
Camping, Zarauz.
1. How many days' accommodation does it cover?
2. The total bill comes to only 100 pesetas. How did they
arrive at this sum?

19 On the waterfront in Javea is the Bar Mediterráneo.
Look at the house next door.
1. Would you normally:
   a) expect to collect your pension from here?
   b) live here permanently?
   c) stay overnight here?
2. Do you enter it by a subway or a staircase?

CLASES	Precio
Helado de corte	7" Pts.
Bombón helado	12"
Cono n.º 1	3
Cono n.º 3	5
Barquillo	7"
Polo de vainilla	5"
" " chocolate	5"
" " fresa	3
" " limón	3
" " naranja	3
Barra de corte 30 x 7 x 7	80

HELADOS FUENTES R. D. G. S. SORIA

OBLEAS

20

1. What sort of business is this?
2. What is the name of the business?
3. Can you get strawberry flavoured ices here?
4. Can you get coffee ice-cream?
5. What will you pay for a tub and two large ice cream cornets?
6. What would be the best buy for the family for tea?

21

It has been raining most of the day. You are in a small square surrounded by rose gardens and very fed up.

1. Which building would you enter if you were also:
   a) sleepy?
   b) thirsty?
2. What does Sr. Bernal sell?
3. What does Sr. Vidal sell?

22 You have spent the morning doing a tour of the town and need a snack.

1. Which of the following can you buy from this kiosk?
   a) vanilla ice-cream
   b) hamburgers with onions and tomato
   c) coffee ice-cream cornets
   d) coca-cola
   e) raspberry water ices
   f) ham sandwiches
   g) hot dogs
2. How much is a hamburger?

23 You have found the Bar Mariñela in old San Sebastián, and eaten well there.

1. What sort of bar is it?
2. Choose what you would like for a two course lunch.
3. What other dishes could you have chosen?
4. Is it just opening or just closing?

24 From the bill of the Fonda Lorca:
1. What is the full address?
2. Name the three main services supplied.
3. To which service does the bill apply?
4. Write the date in full in Spanish.

FONDA
RESTAURANTE

LORCA
Servicio de Taxi

Teléfono 35   PUENTE LA REINA (Navarra)   Mayor, 54

D. _____   DEBE:

Mes	Dia	10 de 9 de 19 70	Pesetas	Cts.
		Una Sopa	15	
		1 de Costillas	60	
		1 de Melocotón	15	
		Vino	10	
			110	

"Casa Florencio"
FONDA
COMIDAS
Amós Olivares, 30 - Teléfono 74

CONCEPTO	Precio
Sopa	2t
Judías	
Paella	
Guisantes con jamón	
Alcachofas con jamón	
Tortilla de gambas	
» » jamón	
» » patatas	
Huevos fritos	
Chuleta de cordero	50
» » cerdo	
Ternera	
Pescados	
Postre	7 5
Vinos	
Cerveza	
Agua mineral	
Pan	3
Café . . . . 2 .	12
Copa	
Cama	6 6
TOTAL	157

Pedro Muñoz, 3 de .... de 1971

25 The Casa Florencio is another typical small *fonda*. As you can see you will find it at 30 Amós Olivares Street. But:
1. In which town?
2. Although you had been travelling all day you were still not very hungry. What did your meal consist of?
3. It cost you 97 pts. What were the 60 pts for?
4. Which of the following could you have chosen from the menu?
   a) artichokes.
   b) Spanish omelette
   c) mushroom omelette
   d) steak
   e) peas
   f) beer
5. What is the significance of *copa*?

Hotel AGUIRRE

Teléfono 24 de ARRE
ORICAIN (Navarra)

Nº 04133

Habitación n.º **11**

Sr. D. *Gregorio Juan Barreiros y Sra.*

Mes de 8 19**75**	Día **23** Pesetas	Día **24** Pesetas	Día......... Pesetas	Día......... Pesetas	Día......... Pesetas	Día......... Pesetas	Día......... Pesetas	TOTALES Pesetas
Habitación	300							
Pens. alimenticia ..								
Desayuno		88						
Almuerzo								
Comida		725						
Pensión								
Total del día ptas. .	300	813						
Suma anterior		300						
Total serv. ordin..		1,113						1,113
Descuento ....%								

26 You are Sr. D. Gregorio Juan Barreiros and you are going on holiday to France. You decide to cross the Pyrenees in daylight and stay the night just outside Pamplona at the Hotel Aguirre.

1. What does *y Sra* mean after your name on the invoice?
2. What cost you 813 pts?
3. For how many people?
4. On what date?
5. A *comida* is a meal. What is an *almuerzo*?
6. How much is 725 pts in sterling at the current rate of exchange?

27 Spanish meals usually have more courses than ours.

1. You feel in the mood for hors d'oeuvres, fish, black pudding and cream caramel. Are they on the menu?
2. Will you get the same menu or a different one if you eat here tomorrow?
3. Pick out one item that is typically English.
4. What is *postre*?
5. Another Englishman is shown to your table as he is having difficulty with the language. Explain what the choices are and what the dishes are like.

```
              MENU DEL DIA

ENTREMESES VARIADOS
GAZPACHO
CONSOME
JUGO DE TOMATE
_____

HUEVOS CON BACON
BONITO AL HORNO
_____

CALLOS A LA MADRILEÑA
POLLO ASADO
MORCILLA DE SORIA
_____                    P O S T R E

FRUTA
FLAN
QUESO
PIÑA
HELADO


Día 20.8.75              Precio 185,- Pts.
```

PROHIBIDO PONER LOS PIES
SOBRE EL LAVABO

28 You are on the move. You want to arrive late and leave early to allow you the maximum travelling time. Accordingly you use camp sites for overnight stops.

1. Does this notice mean:
   a) It is prohibited to wash your feet except in this wash room?
   b) It is prohibited to leave pies and other foodstuffs here?
   c) Do not wash your feet in the basin?
   d) Do not leave taps running?

29 You are staying at the Hotel Alfonso VIII with your parents. This list is on the back of your bedroom door.

1. What is it?
2. What services does it offer for what types of client?
3. You and your parents each send a set of night attire, four handkerchiefs, a set of under clothes and three pairs of socks. As well you need a pair of trousers pressed. If you add a 10% tip what change is there out of a 1000 pts note?
4. Find from a dictionary the meaning of the words you do not know.

PRECIOS

SEÑORA: Lavado y planchado

Camisas noche	25 Pesetas
Bragas	15 »
Sostenes	15 »
Combinaciones	30 »
Pañuelos	8 »
Pijamas	35 »
Blusas	35 »
Sueters	50 »
Faldas	60 »
Vestidos	75 »
Pantalones	70 »

Planchar solamente

Faldas	40 »
Vestidos	45 »
Pantalones	45 »
Abrigos	60 »
Blusas	30 »

CABALLERO: Lavado y planchado

Camisas	35 »
Camisetas	12 »
Pañuelos	8 »
Calcetines	10 »
Pijamas	30 »
Calzoncillos	18 »
Chaquetas	80 »
Pantalones	75 »
Sueters	60 »
Corbatas	15 »

Planchar solamente

Abrigos	90 »
Pantalones	60 »
Chaquetas	60 »
Traje completo	95 »
Corbatas	10 »

30 You are sitting in a café sipping coca cola and you notice this silver cylinder which is ringed with a gold band between two red ones. It is standing on the pavement.

1. Will it be of any use to you on holiday?
2. Will it be as useful to you at 8 pm?
3. For what articles is it designed?

31 You are in a small hill spa called Arnedo above the Ebro valley in Navarra and see this sign.

1. Does this mean:
   a) They sell straps, belts and shoe-laces here?
   b) It is where you pay your rates?
   c) It is a post office?
   d) You can enter here for races?
   e) It is the entrance to the mud baths?
   f) It is a betting shop for the benefit of visitors?
2. While you are deciding this, your friend has been talking to Angelito, the owner of the *peluquería*. About what, do you think?

32 The girl on this kiosk poster is telling you to follow the shortest route.
1. What is the shortest route referred to?
2. What good will it do you if you are stranded in a place you do not know and the last bus has just gone?

33 A message is waiting for you at the *pensión*. Will you please telephone the theatre as soon as possible about some tickets you have booked for tonight.

From the instructions in the telephone box:
1. Is there any particular coin you must use?
2. Will any other value of coin do instead?
3. How long a conversation can you buy for 3 pts?
4. What happens to your money if the line to the theatre is engaged? In Spain do you:
   a) lose your 3 pts?
   b) have the money returned to you?
5. Make a summary of the vital actions you follow when making a local call on a Spanish telephone.

FUNCIONA UNICAMENTE CON MONEDAS DE PESETA

INSTRUCCIONES

* Descuelgue el microteléfono, y una vez oída la señal para marcar, introduzca por la ranura de la parte superior izquierda 3 o 6 monedas de peseta. No se deben introducir más de 6 monedas a la vez. A medida que el aparato vaya cobrando monedas, puede ir reponiendo las percibidas.

* A continuación marque el número deseado.

* Al contestar el número llamado se producirá el cobro de 3 monedas de peseta y comenzará a contarse el primer período de conversación de 3 minutos.

* Momentos antes de finalizar cada período sucesivo de 3 minutos percibirá una tonalidad de aviso y seguidamente se verificará el cobro de otras 3 monedas de peseta o la desconexión automática si se han cobrado todas las introducidas en el aparato.

* Al finalizar la conversación, las monedas de peseta no cobradas le serán devueltas al colgar el microteléfono.

* Si el abonado llamado no contesta o está comunicando, al colgar el microteléfono le serán devueltas igualmente las monedas de peseta introducidas.

* Podrá conversar sin interrupción mientras vea monedas a través del visor.

El precio de la conferencia urbana de 3 minutos o fracción es de TRES pesetas.

34 This notice and kiosk are on the quayside.

1. What are the two ladies buying for their children and themselves?
   a) ice cream
   b) trips round the bay
   c) drinks of beer and pop
   d) keepsakes of San Sebastián
   e) a bus tour of the town
2. Is Aguila the name of a brewery or the owner of the kiosk?
3. How much change will the ladies get from a 500 pts note after they have paid for themselves and their children?

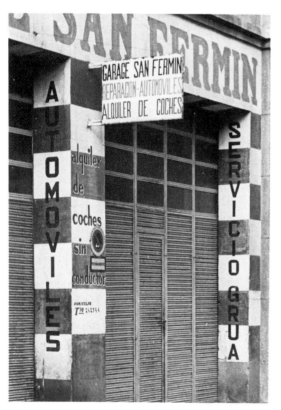

35 You have just arrived in Pamplona and have run out of petrol. You see the Garage San Fermín.

1. Can you get petrol here?
2. What services are advertised?

36 You are travelling fast and fuel consumption is 3 gallons per hour. You decide to top up the tank on the way as you are approaching a barren region which will probably not have many service stations.

1. You choose *super*. What is *gasolina*?
2. What does '96 N.O.' mean?
3. Read the meter. If the total amount of fuel taken up costs 500 pts:
    a) How many litres have you bought?
    b) What is the price per litre?

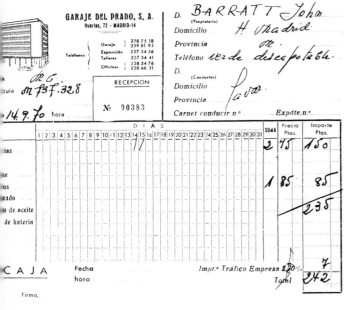

37 This invoice was presented for payment to John Barratt Esq.

1. For what services?
2. When?
3. For what vehicle?
4. With what registration number?
5. What are the other 4 services listed?
6. What are the extra 7 pts on the bill for?

1046.3

SALIDA

38 You will usually see somewhere on Spanish railway stations a number with a short line underneath. The number is different for each station.

1. To what does it refer?
   a) maximum platform weight
   b) date of construction
   c) the town's population
   d) altitude
   e) telephone number of the station
   f) flood level in centimetres
2. What does the poster which refers to cereals (wheat, barley, etc.) advertise?
3. There is a door marked SALIDA. Is it an entrance or an exit?

39 You are leaving Soria for Pamplona at 18.03.

1. Does this time-table refer to:
   a) a bus service?
   b) a coach service?
   c) a railway?
   d) a water taxi service?
2. Will you be leaving in the morning or evening?
3. Can you travel first class?
4. What type of service is it — a through service or one that stops everywhere?
5. Is there likely to be a connection for any other place?
6. If so, where might it be?

Renfe HORARIO SALIDAS

HORA	MINUTOS	CLASE DE TREN	DESTINO	COCHES	OBSERVACIONES
		DIRECCION	CASTEJON		
	4	OMNIBUS-FERROB	ZARAGOZA	FERROBUS	
16	20	OMNIBUS	CASTEJON	2'	
18	03	RAPIDO TER	PAMPLONA BILBAO	1'-2' RTE	
		DIRECCION	TORRALBA		
	6 20	FERROBUS	MADRID	FERRO BUS	
12	03	OMNIBUS	MADRID	2'	
18	05	RAPIDO TER	MADRID	1'-2' RTE.	
18	40	FERROBUS	MADRID	FERROBU	

40

1. What are 'LLEGADAS'?
2. You are expecting a friend to arrive to join you on holiday. She will be travelling as cheaply as possible. Which trains will you meet?
3. If you wanted to go to Madrid, would you find a likely train from this board?

DE TRENES
LLEGADAS

HORA	MINUTOS	CLASE DE TREN	PROCEDENCIA	COCHES
		DIRECCION	CASTEJON	
1	3 2	OMNIBUS	CASTEJON	2ª
1 8	0 2	RAPIDO TER	BILBAO PAMPLONA	1ª-2ª RTE.
2 1	3 0	FERROBUS	ZARAGOZA	FERROBUS
		DIRECCION	TORRALBA	
1 1	1 0	OMN-FERROBUS	MADRID	FERROBUS
1 6	1 4	OMNIBUS	MADRID	2ª
1 7	5 9	RAPIDO TER	MADRID	1ª-2ª RTE.
2 2	2 4	FERROBUS	MADRID	FERROBUS

41

You are going to collect a parcel which has been sent to you by rail and you can see it on the trolley there on the platform.

1. Which door will you go through to claim your parcel?
2. What would you be doing if you were behind the other door?
3. How does the message on the poster try to influence you to buy brandy?

42 You haven't yet bought your tickets for the trip to Pamplona. You are thinking about it while shopping in the town centre. You notice a bus outside a RENFE 'shop'. Nearby is a notice which reads:—

RESERVADO COCHES. DESPACHO CENTRAL.

1. What implication does this have for you?
    a) You are at a bus station.
    b) You are outside a suburban railway station.
    c) You are in a bus park.
    d) You have found a railway booking office.
    e) You are trespassing.
2. What does SP stand for?

43 The notice on the door says that tickets are being sold.

1. What sort of tickets?
2. What does RENFE stand for?
3. Is the office open now as you read this?
4. Which bus will get you to the station in time for you to catch your 18.03 train to Pamplona?
5. When does the office close:
    a) in the evening?
    b) for lunch?
6. When is the office closed all day?

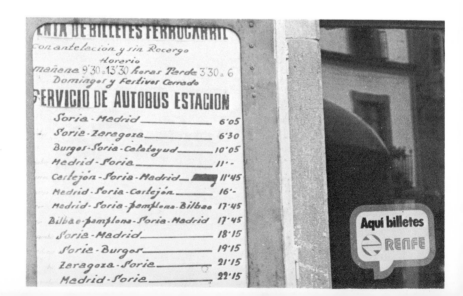

44 *Tabacaleras* are State-owned kiosks, each with their own serial number.
1. Can you name just 2 things they may sell?
2. S.A. means *Sociedad Anónima*. What is the English equivalent of these words?

45 You have been taking a lot of photographs and now unfortunately you have run out of colour film.
1. Will you be able to get a fresh supply from any of the shops here?
2. Is there likely to be a variety to choose from?
3. Will the same shop be able to provide you with ideas for presents to take home?
4. Name 2 of these ideas.
5. What would you use *timbres* for?

46

1. Can I buy a pair of shoes and a shirt from any of these shops?

2. What is Sr. Roldán's profession?

3. A *pastelería* sells *pasteles* and *tartas*. What is a *pastelería*?

47 Would you shop at Ruiz's or Gallardo's for the following articles:

a) a suitcase
b) .22 pellets?
c) a wallet?
d) a present to take home?

e) *chorizo*?
f) fish flies?
g) cheese?
h) a replacement watch strap?
i) *paella* pans?

j) clothes pegs?
k) yoghurt?
l) 500 grams of butter?
m) a wine skin?
n) wine?

48 The Casa Megino in Soria is having a *liquidación de precios*.

1. What does this mean?
2. One old lady looks as though she's seen it all before but a man seems to be rushing to the entrance. What might he be buying?
3. What tells you the time of year?

49 There is a sale on. You decide to go in and look.

1. What is on sale according to the placards?
   a) rope-soled sandals
   b) shoes
   c) slippers
   d) wedges
   e) platforms
2. Will they suit:
   a) men?
   b) women?
   c) teenagers?
   d) children?
3. Are you likely to get 10% off your bill if you buy six pairs? How can you tell?

50 You are window shopping in Logroño until the banks reopen. In the window of Sancarlos are some curtains.
1. Is Sancarlos part of a large network of shops or is it a small family business?
2. Is there any indication that they sell things other than curtains?
3. What special service is it that Sancarlos offers you?
4. By whom is it carried out?
5. How much will it cost to take advantage of this offer?

Sancarlos
cadena textil

Le ofrece
gratuitamente
la instalación de cortinas,
moquetas y rieles por
personal especializado
de la casa

51 Next to Raquel's is a shop.
1. Is 'Viajes' the owner's name or does it advertise some product or other?
2. Name 2 things you can buy from this shop.
3. You want to make a day trip to Segovia. Can you buy the tickets from here?
4. You urgently need some copies of your camera insurance. How long will you have to wait for them?
5. Eugene Products probably supplied the business plate for Raquel. If you went in, what could you get of the following?
   a) a brush and comb set   e) a shave
   b) a shampoo   f) a manicure
   c) perfume   g) a facial
   d) hair styling

52 It is high summer as you pass this building site. The year is 1975.

1. Where are you?
2. Are the builders on target?
3. How long does the National Plan run?
4. Who is the sponsor of this plan?
5. Who has financed the project?
6. What are the 19 units mentioned?
7. What is the name of the Clerk of Works?
8. What function has Don Angel Coronado Castillo?

53

1. How many different trades or professions can you find from these name plates?
2. You are calling on Sr. D. Agustín Alesanco for professional reasons. Might you have:
   a) ingrowing toe-nails?
   b) halitosis?
   c) a divorce pending?
   d) an audition?
   e) TB?
   f) a crumpled suit?
3. Does J. Moreno sell ashtrays and other smokers' requisites? If not, what does he do for a living?

54 This man is looking intently into the shop window.
1. What kind of shop does the sign above his head say it is?
2. He seems to be looking at articles of silver. Can you find any other clue that suggests that the shop does in fact sell silver?
3. What else is sold here?

55 You have come to collect your watch.
1. Why is it just as well you are not taking in a watch for repair but collecting one?
2. For what reason is this?
3. It is 4 o'clock on Tuesday afternoon. Is the shop open?
4. If you went to the shop before 1st October you might find it closed. When would this be?

56 These signs are on the side of a small delivery van. The circular plate indicates that the van is registered in Zaragoza for the carriage of certain goods.

1. Which goods?
2. What sort of *bebidas*?
3. Where is the business carried on?
4. What is the name of the business?

57 This man, ignored by all the bystanders except his wife, is apparently trying to get through the barred gates.

1. Do:
   a) the barrels
   b) the crates
   give a clue to the Rivera business?
2. What two sides to the business are there?

58 You have just spent 76 pts on a ¼ kilo of *champiñones* and 2 kilos of *plátanos*.
  1. Do *champiñones* grow:
     a) on trees?
     b) in the ground?
     c) on bushes?
     d) in water?
  2. What are *plátanos*? (They are yellow and do not grow in Spain).

59 Four people are approaching a chain store. One of the ladies is carrying a bag.
  1. What kind of store is it?
  2. If *embutir* means literally to stuff or to pack, what are *embutidos*?
  3. What might they be buying for lunch? Try making a list in Spanish.

60

1. Who owns this lorry?
2. What is his business?
3. Where is it to be found?
4. In which province?
5. Where was the vehicle registered? (The first two letters will give you a clue).
6. What does *isotermo* tell you?

61

1. What is a *carnicería*?
2. There is a notice that says 'Pollos — 88 pts kilo.' Can you work out whether this is more or less than at your local shop?
3. How many of the animals from the list below are represented in the larger notice?

   a) pig   f) turkey
   b) horse   g) whale
   c) deer   h) lamb
   d) rabbit   i) sheep
   e) pheasant   j) calf

62 You would like to buy your landlady a small present.

1. Do you think *claveles* would be suitable?
2. Would 30 pts worth be sufficient?
3. You have 20 pesetas change and spend them here. What do you buy? What quantity do you get?

63 The lady in front of you paid:
25 pts for 1 k *uvas*
18 pts for ½ k *pimentos*
34 pts for 2 k *tomates*

1. What did she buy?
2. Can you name in Spanish the other article on sale in the picture?

64 This lady will have to look elsewhere as the Autoservicio Pérez is closed.

1. One sign that we are used to seeing in England tells what sort of shop it is. What is it?
2. Will you be served by assistants or will you be obliged to serve yourself?
3. What other products are likely to be sold here?
4. Would you come to this shop to buy a comb and shampoo?

65 A few doors further on is a fishmonger's shop where you notice some ***truchas*** which might suit your friends' palates.

1. What are ***truchas***?
2. How many kilos do you buy?
3. They are 155 pts a kilo. How much will you pay for them?
4. What is the name in Spanish for this type of shop? (To give you a clue, ***pescado*** means fish.)

66

While you are in Spain you are determined to learn to swim.

1. What can the Miniclub help you to do?
2. Can you learn to water-ski there?
3. What is forbidden, where and when?
   a) nude sun-bathing in the summer on the beach.
   b) exercising dogs between certain hours on the beach.
   c) setting up tents on the beach during peak hours.
   d) dropping litter into the sea at high tide.

67

You are going to a bullfight in Olite.

1. Is your seat number 20 or 178?
2. Is this a seat close to the action or far away from it?
3. If the weather remains hot and sunny, what tells you that this is a good location?
4. The advert for Super Ser includes radiators, cookers, washing machines and *estufas*. Can you guess the English word for these?

68 During a morning's sightseeing in San Sebastián you pass by these notices. It is 11 am.

1. What is the building used for?
2. Is it open?
3. What time in the evenings does it close?
4. How much will it cost an adult to go in?
5. Something is advertised to happen at 6 pm.
   a) What is it?
   b) When can you see this?

69

1. Which is true? You are at a:
   a) lunatic asylum
   b) hospital
   c) church
   d) convent
   e) prison
   f) art gallery
   g) museum
   h) historical site
2. What is it that costs 25 pts?
3. Is there a reduction for children between 10 and 13½ years of age?
4. When is the best time in the afternoon to arrive?

41

70 The Coliseum Cinema is showing the film *7 Muertos en el Ojo del Gato.*

1. Can you go this evening?
2. Will they allow in your 16 year old brother?
3. What sort of film is it:
   a) a romance?
   b) a farce?
   c) a thriller?
   d) a murder story?
4. Can you think of an alternative title for it?
5. Some cinemas display notices saying *refrigerado* or *aire acondicionado*. Would you favour these to cinemas without such notices? Why?

71 This man is booking seats at the Cine Rex for tonight's performance.

1. When do you think the times of the performances are?
2. What choice of seats does he have?
3. How close to the screen will he be if he books *plateas*?

72 You are going for a dip but just before you enter the water you see this notice.

1. It applies to both men and women with . . . . what?
2. What must these people not do:
   a) bathe in the nude?
   b) bathe in other than a one-piece costume?
   c) bathe without first paying?
   d) bathe without showering?
   e) bathe without a bathing cap?

73 This year in August you go to Santander for your holiday. The local Oficina de Información y Turismo is glad to tell you about the Santander Festival.

1. When will it be possible to see a play?
2. Much of the advertised entertainment is foreign. You would like to see something Spanish. What choice do you have?
3. You have heard concerts broadcast from Spain by the national station. Might you be able to attend a live performance whilst you are in Santander?
4. What Eastern Bloc countries are represented?
5. How many different kinds of show are being presented during the festival?

74 This is your ticket to the Cine Coliseum in Madrid.

1. For which performance is it?
2. On which date?
3. Will you be sitting downstairs or upstairs?
4. Will it be a good seat?
5. Can you choose your own seat when you get inside?

75 You are the manager of this dodgem car track.

1. There are six cars on the track, so what is your total take this time?
2. How do your customers pay?
3. A tourist reports the loss of a fountain pen. He is sure that he lost it on the track. What is your reaction?
4. Does the notice say that you must not bump other cars?
5. You notice an adult passenger in a car with a child. They are not complying with your safety requirement. What is this?

76 The Iglesia de la Vera-Cruz is an historical monument, one of the very many in Segovia.

1. What is it:
   a) a church?
   b) a farmhouse fortified against the Moors?
   c) an inland lighthouse?
   d) a hermit's look-out?
2. Who built it?
3. How does it say that your 10 pts entrance fee will be used?

IGLESIA DE LA VERA-CRUZ O DE LOS TEMPLARIOS

SEGOVIA

Nº 003781

El importe de esta recaudación se destina a la conservación del templo, culto y obras benéficas de la Orden de Malta.

10 pesetas

FIESTAS PATRONALES - Olite

PROGRAMA de Festejos organizados por el Club
ERRI-BERRI

Día 13

A las 5 y cuarto gran partido de Fútbol entre los

equipos **HURACAN F. C. - ERRI-BERRI**
(DE ALLO)

Día 17

A las 5 de la tarde, Extraordinaria Novillada, en la que serán lidiados 2 NOVILLOS por los aficionados de la localidad.

José Julián Eraso Erro (Caracoles)
y Angel Lacarra Luna (Gatera)

con sus correspondientes cuadrillas **(PRECIOS POPULARES)**.

A continuación de la Novillada, chavales infantiles jugarán un partido de fútbol con dos novillas en el ruedo; el equipo vencedor obtendrá un gran Premio.

Día 19

A las 5 y media de la tarde partido de Fútbol entre los equipos Juveniles,

Peña Sport - Erri-Berri

Día 21

Para finalizar las fiestas, GRAN VERBENA a beneficio del Club, en colaboración con la Sala «El Castillo»

¡¡OLITENSES!!
Colaboremos con nuestro Club

IMP. GOLDARACENA. - TAPALLA

---

77 You are in Olite in fiesta week. It is going to be very enjoyable, as you can see from this bill of events.

1. Who has arranged the programme?
2. What are they?
3. Look at the programme for the 17
   a) What sort of event is it?
   b) Who might Caracoles and Gatera be?
   c) Are they amateur or professional
   d) Would you expect them to be well known to the spectators?
   e) What do you think a *cuadrilla* is
   f) Can you find out what the word *novillada* means?
   g) Will you expect to pay a lot or a little for your ticket?
   h) At what time of day do activities begin?
4. The fiestas end with a *Gran Verbena*. What is that?

78 A passer-by stops you and asks your opinion on some information in this poster.

1. He has heard of D. Angel Peralta but is not really sure who he is. Who is he?
2. How does he differ in what he does from El Cordobés?
3. On what dates can you see:
   a) El Cordobés, and
   b) The Peraltas, in action?
4. Is there any indication that D. Clemente Tassara's bulls are different from those of the Nuñez brothers?

PLAZA DE TOROS

CORDOBA

Empresa: VALENCIA

Con motivo de la FERIA DE MAYO 1.971, durante los días **25, 26, 27, 29 y 30** se celebrarán, patrocinados por el Excmo. Ayuntamiento con permiso de la Autoridad y si el tiempo no lo impide,

Grandes Acontecimientos Taurinos, 5

Martes, 25.	Jueves, 27.
GRANDIOSA CORRIDA DE TOROS;	**¡¡Gran Corrida del Arte del Rejoneo!!**
SEIS magníficos Toros, SEIS	SEIS Magníficos y Bravos TOROS, SEIS
Divisa blanca y azul. Señal: Rajadas las dos orejas en forma de pendiente. Ganadería de	Divisa: Verde y amarilla. Señal: Brincada en ambas orejas, de la afamada ganadería de
NUÑEZ HERMANOS	D. CLEMENTE TASSARA
De Tarifa- (Cádiz.) ESPADAS:	de MADRID. Para los cuatro jinetes del apoteósis,
antiago Martín EL VITI	D. Angel **Peralta** ▪ D. Rafael **Peralta**
MANUEL BENITEZ	
EL CORDOBES	
lorencio Casado EL HENCHO	D. Alvaro **Domecq** ▪ D. José M. **Lupi**
con sus cuadrillas de picadores y banderilleros.	Con sus cuadrillas de auxiliadores y sobresalientes.

5. You are now in deep conversation with your new friend. He notices that both the *espadas* and the horsemen have *cuadrillas.*
   a) Can you explain this term?
   b) Why are three of the matadors called *espadas*?

6. What might they be doing by late evening on 27th May?

7. What could put an end to the bullfight advertised?

8. Which bullfight do you think will be more popular — the one on Tuesday or the one on Thursday. Why?

79 This sign prohibits entry to whom?

a) everybody
b) only those who speak Spanish
c) people with no business there
d) all persons next to the notice

80 You are on the outskirts of Zarauz. The holidaymaker in shorts has just asked you what the sign means.

1. Did you tell him:
   a) that the Savings Banks in Zarauz were to be found at the five places shown underneath?
   b) that those were the only churches open for worship during the summer season?
   c) that it was a list of the monasteries and convents in the town?
   d) that it was a list of buildings of tourist interest?
2. What does the S followed by roman numerals mean?

81 This sign is by a stone fountain outside a village.

1. Does it say that the water may be used for:
   a) taking away?
   b) cooking?
   c) drinking?
   d) washing
   e) washing up?
   f) animals?

82 On the approaches to villages and small towns you will sometimes come across a sign like this.

1. At what time is evensong?
2. What are the morning services called? When are they?
3. Would you expect to attend a:
   a) Catholic
   b) Church of England
   c) Protestant
   d) Muslim
   e) Baptist
   f) Free Church service here?

83 Here you have information regarding all the church services available in Soria.

1. On what days are services?
2. Can you attend a 7.30 Sunday morning service at which the Carmelite Fathers officiate?
3. How has the information been divided to make it easier for the reader?
4. Your parents would like to attend the cathedral service on Sunday morning. What choice of services do they have?
5. You decide eventually to go to the 8.30 mass. Where is one being held?
6. Can you think of a meaning for PP. and RR.PP.?

HORARIO DE MISAS EN SOI

LOS DIAS DE PRECEPTO

SÁBADOS POR LA TARDE
y vísperas de fiestas

Hora	Templo.
6	San Francisco - (Antiguo Hospital).
6,30	S. I. Catedral de S. Pedro.
7	San Juan de Rabanera.
	PP. Escolapios.
7,30	PP. Carmelitas.
	PP. Franciscanos.
8	Santa María La Mayor.
	El Salvador.

Domingos y festivos

(Por Iglesias)

S. I. CATEDRAL DE SAN PEDRO
9, 10'30, 11'30, mañana
y 6'30 tarde.

RR. PP. CARMELITAS
8, 9, 10, 11, 12'30, 1'30 mañana
y 7'30 tarde.

PARROQUIA DE NTRA. SRA. DEL ESPINO

Domingos y festivos. - (Po
Por la mañana

7,30	PP. Escolapios.
8	PP. Carmelitas.
	Siervas de Jesús.
8,30	Santa María La Mayor.
	PP. Escolapios.
	PP. Franciscanos.
9	S. I. Catedral de San Pedro.
	PP. Carmelitas.
	San Juan de Rabanera.
	El Salvador.
	San José (solo en verano).
9,30	Santa María La Mayor.
	PP. Escolapios.
	PP. Franciscanos.
	San Francisco de Asis - (Antiguo Hos
10	Ntra. Sra. del Espino.
	PP. Carmelitas.
	Santo Domingo.
	El Salvador.
	San José (Barriada de Yagüe). (En a las 9).
	Ermita de San Saturio (solo en vera
10,30	S. I. Catedral de S. Pedro.
	Santa María La Mayor.
	PP. Franciscanos.
	PP. Escolapios.

84 You've spent a good morning looking round the Alcázar and sight-seeing generally. Passing by a square you notice this sign to a WC. Just what you need.

1. Does it cost adults 500 pts to use the WC? Do children have to pay?
2. Something is prohibited. Is it:
   a) entry to the garden?
   b) watering the flowers?
   c) using the hedge as a toilet?
   d) sticking large or small bills on the wall?
3. Is there a fine if you are caught?

85

1. This is the sign for a National . . . . Reserve. You supply the missing word.
2. What things are you likely to find here?
3. The notice in the distance says something about a fire. What is it?
4. What is a *colilla*?
5. What is it you should not do with one?
6. Are you allowed to go fishing?
7. More usual are the many small wayside signs that say *coto de caza* or *coto de pesca* or more simply *coto*. How do you think these differ from the National Reserve?
8. What is a *coto*?

86

You are moving west across Old Castile.

1. If you stayed on the Camino de Santiago where would you end up?
2. Is this road old or quite new?
3. Who would have used it in days gone by?
4. Where might they have rested?
5. What does 'S.XIII' mean?
6. If you followed the road through Spain what might one of your interests be?

Camino de Santiago

Valdefuentes

Ermita de Santiago S.XIII
Antigua ruta de peregrinos

87

1. Would you place in this container:
   a) letters?
   b) spectacles?
   c) litter?
   d) prescriptions?
   e) films for processing?
   f) old bus tickets?
2. Why is Martínez Terrel's name on the box? Is he the dustman?
3. What three kinds of the same thing does he offer?
4. How would you find him?

88

The coat of arms is of Navarra. The sign itself is sited at a lay-by in an unspoiled beauty spot in the hills. The views are extensive, and most people stop to look.

1. What is the general theme of the notice?
2. Why do you think it might be successful?

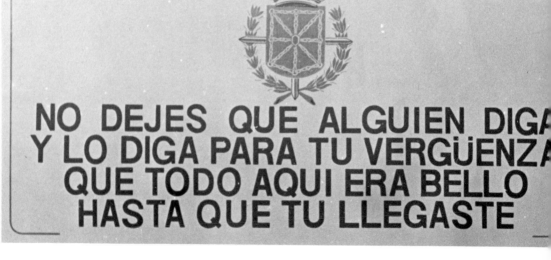

89 It is the 12th July. You hear a cry in the Street: *¡Sale hoy!*, *¡Sale hoy!* and notice this poster for the National Lottery.

1. What importance has 12th July?
2. How much money is being given away in prizes?
3. You have a fling, keep your fingers crossed and buy a ticket for 500 pts.
   a) What sort of ticket is it?
   b) How much would you need to pay for a whole ticket?
   c) How much is this in pounds and pence?

TOPICS

	Picture Number
Road and Traffic Signs	*1-17*
Information	2-10, 14, 15, 16
Instructions	6, 9, 11-13, 15, 16
Parking and Blue Zone	1, 13, 15-17
Accommodation and Food	*18-29*
Camping	18, 28
Hotel	26, 29
Pensión	19, 21
Restaurants	23-26, 27
Ice cream	20, 22
Other refreshment	21, 23
Communications	*30-33*
Transport	*34-43*
Boat	34
Car and Garage	35-37
Railway Station	38, 41
Train timetables	39, 40, 43
Shops — General	*44-55*
Sale time	48, 49
Shops — Food and Drink	*56-65*
Pastimes	*66-78*
Bulls	67, 77, 78
Cinema, theatre	70, 71, 73, 74
Fairground	75
Football	77
Sightseeing	68, 69, 76
Swimming	66, 72
General Notices	*79-89*
Information	80-87, 89
Prohibition	79, 84, 85, 88

LANGUAGE PATTERNS

	Picture Number
a with distance and place where	5, 8
a with warning	10
a with infinitive	18
addresses	24, 25, 37, 87
adjectives — agreement	1, 14, 27, 32, 86, 87, 89
adjectives — position	27, 32, 34, 48, 86
adjectives used with a noun	1
al with infinitive	33
article omitted with preposition	10, 11
article with dates, times	55, 77
con in place of 'and'	25, 27
dates — use of *día*	73, 77
familiar form of address	11, 88
hay meaning 'on sale'	23
imperative — familiar form	11
imperative — infinitive	75
imperative — past participle with infinitive	13, 28, 72
imperative — subjunctive	15, 33, 75, 85, 88
neuter *lo*	88
para with infinitive ('in order to')	77
para meaning 'intended for'	17, 38, 87
por meaning 'by' (agent)	50, 77
por meaning 'on' (place)	11
por meaning 'per' (proportion)	18, 36, 69
por meaning 'in' (time)	55
pronoun — relative	77
use of the reflexive *se*	66, 76, 84
subjunctive with adverbial clause	17
subjunctive with verb of permission	88
subjunctive with possibility	17, 33
time without definite article	1, 13

WORD LIST

The meanings given are specific to the context of the pictures. Other meanings have been generally omitted.

Sometimes you will come across a box in which you will find a selection of words related in topic. You may find these useful in widening your appreciation of this topic.

abono subscription, guarantee
aceite oil
acera pavement
acontecimiento event
en al acto while you wait
aficionado fan, enthusiast
aguas menores urine, water
aguas mayores faeces, excrement
ahumado smoked
ajeno not of, having no business with
alcachofa artichoke
alguien anyone
alimentación food
almacén store, warehouse
almuerzo lunch, snack

---

desayuno breakfast
comida meal, lunch, midday meal
cena supper, dinner in the evening
causeo snack
merienda tea-time snack
bocadillos filled bread rolls
sandwiches filled bread slices
platos combinados in Spain meat and vegetables are taken separately. If they are eaten together on one plate as in England, they are known as *platos combinados*
bolsa de viaje packed lunch
postre sweet course, dessert
tapas appetisers eaten with a drink.

---

alquiler to hire
anisado aniseed drink
antelación priority
aparcamiento parking
aparejador overseer, Clerk of Works
arreglo arrangement, order
atún tunny fish
ayuntamiento town hall

banderillero the man who places the darts in the bull during a bullfight
bañarse to bathe
barquillo large square section cornet of ice cream
besugo sea bream (carp)
bocadillo filled bread roll
bombón helado choc ice
bonito striped tunny fish
braza breast stroke
butaca front stall seat

cadena chain
calamares squid
calentador heater
calzados footware
callos tripe
cambio change, exchange
camión lorry, truck
carga charge up
carnet de conductor driving permit
carnicería butcher's shop

carrocería coachbuilder's works

caza game, hunting

cenicero ashtray

cerdo pork

claustro cloister

clavel carnation

cobrar to charge for, to cover

cocina cooker, kitchen

coches sin conductor self-drive hire cars

colgar to hang up

colilla cigarette end

colocar to arrange, to place

confecciones household linen

cono cornet (ice cream)

cordero lamb

correos the post

correr to run

corrida bullfight of mature bulls

---

novillada bullfight with young bulls and apprentice bullfighters

becerrada usually an amateur fight with very young bulls, 1 to 2 years old

rejoneo bullfight from horseback with a *rejón* or short lance

alguaciles mounted bailiffs who receive the keys of the bull pens from the president of a bullfight at the start of a fight

matador a formal killer of bulls sometimes called an *espada*

estoque sword

pica lance carried by mounted picador

banderilla steel pointed dart placed in the bull's shoulder during a bullfight by the *banderillero*

cuadrilla team of helpers consisting of *picadores, banderilleros* and general helpers (*monosabios*)

paseo formal entry into ring at the start of a *corrida*

sorteo draw to find which bulls will be

---

fighting which matador

sobresaliente substitute

traje de luces fighting suit

capote silk fighting cape

muleta red cloth used in final act

quite the separation of bull from horse or man by using the cape

orejas ears

rabo tail

suerte a corrida consists of 3 *suertes* or *tercios* (thirds); *s. de varas* (lances); *s. de banderillas; s. de la muerte*

---

cortinas curtains

costillas chops

coto area, terrain

cuadrilla a matador's team of helpers

cuñas wedge heeled shoes

curtidos leather goods

champiñón mushroom

charcutería shop selling prepared meats

chaval (-a) lad (lass)

chipirones small version of calamares or squid

chorizo highly seasoned smoked sausage

chuleta cutlet

decimo tenth part (of a lottery ticket)

dejar to leave, let

descuento discount

devolver to refund

dirección address (*domicilio* and *señas* are also used in this context)

divisa emblem

dna (docena) dozen

domicilio home

domingo Sunday

embutido stuffed, packed

empresa enterprise, business

enfermedad illness

engrase greasing

entremeses hors d'œuvres
entresuelo mezzanine

> **planta baja** ground floor
> **piso primero** 1st floor (2nd storey above
> the *entresuelo*)

espada sword, and by implication some-
    times the swordsman
espalda back stroke
estacionamiento car parking
estancia stay
estufa stove
expendeduría shop where monopoly
    goods are sold

fecha date
feria fair
ferretería hardware shop, ironmonger's

> **armería** gunsmith
> **cerrajería** locksmith
> **llaves** keys

ferrocarril railway
festejos entertainment
ficha ticket, card
de frente head on
frigorífico refrigerator

gafas glasses, spectacles
gambas prawns
gazpacho Andalusian cold garlic soup
gorro cap
grúa crane
guisantes peas

helado de corte ice cream wafer
horario time-table
horchata a cooling milk-like drink made
    from almonds
al horno baked

importe amount, total price

jinete horseman
joyería jeweller's shop
judías beans
jueves Thursday
jugo juice

lavadora washing machine
lentillas de contacto contact lenses
lidiar to fight, contest (e.g. bullfight)
local premises
lomo loin
lucha fight, struggle
lugar place
llegada arrival

mantequería dairy
mariposa butterfly (stroke)
a medida que while
mejillones mussels
melocotón, peach, *m. en almíbar*, tinned
    peach
merluza hake
microteléfono telephone handset
Ministerio de la Vivienda Ministry of
    Housing
moqueta fabric used in upholstery
morcilla black pudding
con motivo de on the occasion of
multa fine

natación swimming
novillada bullfight between an apprentice
    matador and young bulls

obras benéficas works of charity

palco box at a theatre or cinema
panadería baker
pañería draper's shop
parabrisas windscreen

pastelería pastry or cake shop
peatón pedestrian
peluquería hairdresser's shop
pensión lodging house, boarding house
pensión alimenticia meals only in a
 pensión
pensión completa full board and lodging
peregrino pilgrim
pez (*pl. peces*) fish
picador horseman with pike in first part
 of a bullfight
pimentos peppers
piña pineapple
plátano banana
platea front stall
platería silversmith's shop
póliza invoice
polo iced lolly
pollo chicken
postre sweet course, dessert
potable drinkable
RP padres, fathers

RP Reverend Father
RR PP Reverend Fathers
S, Sto, Sta Saint
RM Reverend Mother

---

precepto order, rule
preciso necessary
pulpo octopus

queso cheese

ranura slot
rebaja reduction, discount

---

liquidación sale, clearance
ofertas offers
pares sueltos oddments, part items`
restos de serie remnants, ends of lines
surtido stock, supply

---

recargo extra charge or tax

recaudación collection
rejoneador matador who fights from
 horseback with a short lance
relojería watchmaker's shop
RENFE *Red Nacional de Ferrocarriles
 Españoles,* (Spanish National Railway
 Network)

---

expreso normal stopping train
rápido through train with only main
town stops. Some of these are named,
eg *Rápido-TER*
tren ómnibus stopping (or local) train
férrobus one coach train
automotor combined carriage with
driver compartment at each end

---

responder de to be responsible for
riel rail

salchichas sausages
salidas departures
sastrería tailor's shop
sello stamp
señal mark
servicios toilets

---

señoras, damas ladies
señores, caballeros, hombres gents
aseos washroom
orinarios gents only
retrete toilet, lavatory
W.C. as in English but pronounced
'vay-thay'
el water W.C.

---

sillón de entresuelo balcony seat in
 cinema or theatre
sobresaliente substitute for a matador in
 case of accidents
sorteo draw
subida way up

bajada way down
entrada way in
salida way out
ascensor lift

sujetar to hold on

tabacalera tobacconist
taller workshop
taquilla ticket office
tendido one of a row of seats, the row itself
ternera veal
timbre stamp, bell
tortilla omelette
a través de through, across
trucha trout

uvas grapes

vencedor victor, winner
verbena outdoor dance at night on the eve
    of a saint's day
vergüenza shame
vespertina evening service
viaje journey, tour

zapato shoe